Use What You Have To Get What You Want

Other books by **Jack Nadel**

Cracking the Global Market

There's No Business Like Your Business

*How To Succeed In Business Without Lying
Cheating or Stealing*

My Enemy, My Friend

Use What You Have To Get What You Want

100 Basic Ideas That Mean Business

By

JACK NADEL

Edited by Joel Silberman

JNJ Publishing
1482 East Valley Road
Suite 317
Santa Barbara, CA 93108

Library of Congress Control Number: 2010938400

Cover: Pausha Foley
Proof reader: Karen Wilder

www.ideasthatmeanbusiness.com

ISBN 978-0-9846282-0-9

Printed in the United States of America
On acid free, recycled paper

Distributed by
AtlasBooks

To Julie,

My wife, partner and best friend, whose positive attitude and constant care brought me through a life-threatening illness and continues to provide encouragement and inspiration.

In 1978, newly divorced with two young daughters, Julie had to earn enough money to provide for herself and for the education of her children. With her love and talent for food preparation, her detail-oriented mind, and her outgoing personality, catering and event planning became her chosen field.

From high profile celebrity weddings and Hollywood studio parties, to the Super Bowl and the 1984 Olympics Julie built her company, Parties Plus, into a well-recognized and respected organization that was sold to a public company in 1990.

Julie now devotes a great deal of her time to charity work and has a challenging full time job, being married to me.

Contents

Editor's Foreword

Jack Nadel is a true American Original: decorated World War II US Army Air Corps B29 navigator with 27 bombing missions over Japan, self-made global entrepreneur, author, philanthropist, and my dear friend and mentor.

I first met Jack in 1989 while working in the entertainment industry. We became friends and over the years had serious conversations about how I could create a more prosperous life for myself by changing my thinking.

The first thing Jack suggested seemed impossible...*you don't have to learn anything new.* I was living paycheck to paycheck, so I decided to listen to him. And it worked!

Through Jack's wise and patient tutelage, I retooled my thinking and by using his *Basic Ideas That Mean Business,* my life was dramatically changed forever.

Working with him on this book has been a true labor of love, because I know every word of it has worked for me.

Joel Silberman

Author's Introduction

In January of 1946, I was discharged from the U.S. Army Air Corps and entered a post-war commercial world filled with tremendous opportunities. That's when the basic idea, *Find the Need and Fill It*, was created, guiding my next 65 successful years in the world's marketplace. This book starts with that same *basic*, and adds 99 more time-proven *basic ideas that mean business.*

Today, millions of people are unemployed, and are out looking for jobs that are very scarce. Many more millions are working, but their earnings do not equal their expenses. Either they must find better paying jobs, reduce their standards of living, or find a way to augment income.

I believe our problems can best be solved by our own efforts. You have greater capabilities than you think you have, and many of these can be translated into cash at the marketplace. *Use What You Have To Get What You Want* will point the way and give you some *rules of the road* from a well-tested traveler.

A number of people I know have carved new directions for themselves, working within their capabilities, stretching beyond their expectations.

A 42-year old mother of two was laid off from her job of nine years with the Mexican government. After an intensive search she was unable to find another position. One of her greatest pleasures is to bake pastries. She decided to offer her homemade baked goods for sale through her local supermarket. Today she is supplying a number of supermarkets in Mexico out of two locations and has 20 employees. This lady is making more money than she ever made before by re-booting her mind to make her pleasure her business.

A middle-aged woman with chronic gastro-intestinal problems converted her medical handicap and knowledge into online profit. Supported by her satisfied customers, today her Internet following receives daily informational emails and readers are buying her books of special recipes and products. She has developed a business that helps people... *and* makes money.

Use What You Have To Get What You Want shows you how to rethink your skill set. By *owning* these basic ideas and fitting them to your individual needs, you can turn the knowledge that you already possess into a new revenue stream.

These *basics* have been distilled from my 65 years of successful experience in business. Read all 100 carefully, think about them, and then choose those that resonate with you.

Your gut instinct is the most reliable feeling that you have; it is the sum of all of your experiences. Through these *basics* you can create your own path to success and financial freedom. After you have read the entire book, go back and examine them one at a time and you will know what works for you.

The American Dream is best when shared by many. These *basics* are a practical application of a dream that leads us to a fulfilling life. I have always believed that we celebrate our successes and take responsibility for our failures. Do not fear failure – learn from it.

My goal in writing this book is to pass on 100 basic successful ideas that have meant business through the years.

So that we can communicate with each other, and have a place to share our stories, we have a website www.ideasthatmeanbusiness.com. We invite you to blog about *your* experiences, offer advice, and seek help when needed.

I was born in very poor circumstances. I have a high school education, and never went to college.

My conclusion is very simple –
If I can make it ...so can you!

Jack Nadel
July 2010

How To Use This Book To Get What You Want

By reading this book you are taking the first steps in your journey toward *using what you have to get what you want* by retooling your thinking.

To quote an ancient Chinese proverb,

> *Give someone a fish and you feed him for a day.*
> *Teach someone to fish and you feed him for a lifetime.*

Reading this book is learning to fish. The fish have always been there, waiting for you. It's up to you to find them. To do that, you need to determine what the fish want to eat. That's the bait to put on the end of your hook and cast into the water. When they bite, you must have the patience, tenacity and skill to reel them in.

Believe, Absorb, Become

Retooling starts in your mind, truly learning to think a new way. Then, it moves into your being and actions.

First, you must *believe* that the basic ideas that mean business contained in this book can work for you. Then you need to *absorb* these *basics* into your gut so that they truly *become* part of who you are.

When you digest these ideas, you will create the capability of achieving financial success. No two successful people think exactly alike but they share a common attitude and mindset. It is up to you to pick and choose those *basics* that work for you.

The 100 basic ideas you are about to read are proven facts of business life. These facts can become your springboard to a workable business plan that will make you financially secure. When you enjoy financially rewarding work, your goal is in sight.

Assess, Imagine, Play the *What If Game*

- What does success look like for you?
- How does it feel?
- When you see it in your mind does it make you happy?

If your success doesn't feel good, then you must re-examine your goal. A key to lasting financial success is enjoying what you do.

Begin by assessing what you have, making a list of all your training, skills and experiences. Each of these can be the basis for a rewarding career. Armed with this list, give yourself a specified period of time – an hour, two hours, one half-hour (it doesn't matter as long as you specify a timeframe) and play the *What If Game*.

The *What If Game* takes place completely in your mind. To play the *What If Game* all you need is your list of possibilities and your wish list of results. Then you begin to connect the dots. Let me give you an example.

A successful performer, orchestra conductor, producer and theatrical director had spent 20 years in show business without amassing any personal financial stability. I told him, that given the skills he possessed, he didn't need to learn anything new. What he needed to do was use those skills in a new way that provided a sustainable income.

First, he made a list of everything that he was trained to do and capable of doing. In an *out-of-the-box* thinking exercise, connecting the dots of his skills, he discovered he was capable of training different actors – actors who could afford to be trained (politicians and organizational CEOs) – to work in the media and effectively communicate their message.

Joel Silberman is now a successful media consultant and the editor of this book. Joel's turnaround gave him a way forward that is both fulfilling and financially rewarding. This process was the start of *Use What You Have To Get What You Want*.

How Do *You* Use This Book?

When you open the book, open your mind. The ideas presented are deliberately designed to engage your instincts rather than your analysis.

Read it; don't over-think it. We want to retool the way you think. That cannot happen with your old mindset. You must reboot your thinking.

Next, assume it will work. That sounds simple. But sadly, most people are skeptical, and believe that nothing will work. With *100 Basic Ideas That Mean Business*, it will work!

Your attitude is the one thing that you can change today that will change the way you are perceived by everyone else immediately. *Attitude* instantly shifts thinking to the positive. It can and will work for you.

Now...read the book through for the first time. Give yourself the freedom to process what you have read. Some *basic ideas* will resonate with you immediately. These are the ideas to be closely examined and applied to your business plan.

100 Basic Ideas That Mean Business are the result of 65 years of continuous success. They are not theory; they really do work.

Let them work for you.

100 Basic Ideas
That Mean Business

1

Find a need and fill it.

For 65 years of successful business this *basic* has been the reason I started every deal. The greater the need, the greater the potential.

My very first deal:

The Chinese Government was looking for navy blue woolen material to make uniforms. There was none available. There was, however, army olive drab in large quantities for sale at war surplus (WWII). I bought Army olive drab, had it dyed navy, and sold it to the Chinese.

2

Self-motivation is the key to success and will achieve powerful results.

The purpose of these 100 basic ideas that mean business is to achieve power from within that becomes a part of who we are. We can no longer depend on outside forces to give us a better standard of living. Regardless of the economic news, the action of government, or the natural forces that oppose us, we must build within ourselves the capability to survive, prosper, and feel good.

Five years ago I had the first of five knee operations. At that time I hired a caregiver and we seemed to relate to each other from our first conversation. His ability to render necessary services above and beyond what would normally be expected directly affected my health. This caregiver went out of his way to study my work and the books that I had written. He also kept up with the computer technology. This caregiver studied to become a massage therapist and trainer. Today he uses all these skills and is a tremendous asset to me in my work and in my travels. His remarkable motivation came from within and helped him acquire a higher standard of living as he became more valuable.

3

Take calculated risks.

There is no such thing as a deal with *no* risk. The amount of risk is directly proportionate to the gain. When someone offers a deal and says, "You can't lose," it's probably time to walk away.

When we established a pen factory in Europe, everybody said it was too risky and would cost too much money to set up. But, as we already had distribution in the European Common Market (now the EEC), and knew, by manufacturing in the area, that we could improve delivery, reduce prices and get much more business, the odds were definitely with us. The increased business and profit justified the risk. Entering this market was the result of intense research and the knowledge that the value of the American dollar to the European currency is an important factor. It becomes axiomatic that a cheap dollar facilitates export and an expensive dollar makes imports easier.

4

The three R's for successful business are: Relationships, Results and Rewards.

The three R's for basic education are Reading, wRiting and aRithmetic. Without these basics learning becomes almost impossible. In business, it all starts with the relationship. You are judged by the results. And the rewards spring from the results.

In 1988 President Reagan asked me to join a Trade Mission to Japan. The purpose was to sell more American products and help correct an imbalance in trade.

We met with many of the great Japanese industrialists highlighted by a luncheon I had with Akio Morita, the President of Sony. He said, "You Americans come here to make a deal. We Japanese are interested in forming a relationship that would be the starting point of many deals."

During these meetings we forged closer relationships with our Japanese counterparts resulting in increased business and greater understanding. Results and rewards were the dividends from forming those relationships.

5

More deals die from sloppy execution than from bad concepts.

A deal is made verbally and is not confirmed in writing. The result is a misunderstanding and a possible lawsuit. Success depends on an overwhelming attention to detail and a willingness to change direction.

I made a deal to manufacture ballpoint pens in China. The factory was slow and late in delivery. Our warehouse was not properly set up to handle this merchandise and our sales force was not prepared to take advantage of the moment. The concept was great but the execution was poor and the deal died.

6

Understand your strengths and weaknesses.

If you are great in sales but bad with figures, get out and sell. Hire someone else to keep the score.

When starting in business, I had limited time and funds. My selling skills were great, my detail skills were – and still are – terrible. So, I decided to spend money hiring competent people to do the detail work and wound up with more efficiency and greater profit by devoting the major part of my time to selling.

7

Don't fall in love with your idea.

An original idea is usually born with many imperfections. It takes time, effort, and discipline to make it beautiful. Sometimes it never gets there. If you love it, you may not want to let it die. Reserve your love for people.

Our primary business was sales promotion: manufacturing and distributing promotional products. One day an associate convinced us we should be in the hobby business. However, our experience was manufacturing utility items, like ballpoint pens and stationery. Yet, we invested in a hobby company in Minnesota until we suddenly realized this was not the right business for us because we did not really understand or love this business. Before getting in over our heads, we sold our interest, took the loss and happily withdrew.

8

When looking for advice, talk to someone who's done it successfully.

When you consult with a successful veteran of the business you wish to enter, you will get an opinion from someone who has been there and knows the pitfalls as well as the potential. Now you have good advice from which to make your own decision. The odds are you will make the right move.

I had a very successful Uncle who gave me advice on how to invest my profits. He told me, "Use an investment specialist with super research facilities." I followed his advice and my money made money.

9

Do your own research.

When you get information secondhand, it has been filtered through somebody else's prejudices. At least at the beginning, get the facts directly from the source.

One of my division managers strongly recommended that we go into the business of producing trade shows. He gave me statistics that turned out to be false. I did my own research and decided the chances for success were very small in an overcrowded and expensive field and turned the deal down. He resigned, bankrolled his own trade show company and lost his entire investment shortly thereafter.

10

Scale your business plan to fit your ability to finance it. If funds are limited, take it in stages.

Figure your cash projections realistically. The need for cash in various stages of your business is an estimate of great importance. Better to go more slowly at first and build your business in stages. Each successive stage will be easier to finance as you will have a proven track record, making it easier to raise additional funds.

I started Jack Nadel International as a local operation in Southern California. I expanded into other parts of the country and throughout the world only after being successful in the original territory.

11

A great product is one that sells.

There is no such thing as an artistic success in the world of products. There is only one test. If it sells and makes a strong return on your investment (in both time and money), then it is a good product. If it creates a great profit over an extended period, then it is a *super* product.

*We were presented with a watch calendar (an aluminum tab with the calendar of the month wrapped around the wristband in 1975 before the advent of digital watches. I really didn't like the product but, because of a relationship with the person selling it, I sent it to my sales people. I was shocked by the orders we received and ultimately this one product, **that I did not like**, was one of the most profitable products we ever sold. 22 million wristband calendars later...this proved to be a super product!*

12

Sell it before you commit to making it or doing it.

If it's a product, make a sample. If it's a service, sell it in advance.

Tooling a new product and investing in inventory is very expensive. If you can possibly make a handmade prototype, you can pre-sell the product and greatly minimize the risk. If it sells, you can manufacture to the demand. If it doesn't sell, your losses are minimal.

The same principle applies to a new service. Sell the service to some prospects in advance.

My wife had a catering business... basically on-demand in the beginning. She never bought any event specific materials before the contract was signed and she knew she was paid for what would be un-returnable merchandise.

13

Does it work?
Will it last?
Who wants it?

If you can say yes to the first two questions and see a big demand in answer to the third, it's a winner.

Shortly after highlighter pens were introduced to the marketplace, I had the idea to put a highlighter on the opposite end of a regular ballpoint pen. It worked well and the sales were excellent to millions of people that welcomed the convenience of the unique ability of this pen to write and highlight with the same instrument.

14

Great design is when ordinary force produces extraordinary results.

A flute is designed to make wind sound beautiful. But, it doesn't work without special skill. Great design takes the guesswork out of using a product. A service can be continually refined and tailored to the customer's need.

There was a need for a flexible measuring tape to measure the inside diameter of oil pipes. I asked a manufacturer of metal measuring tapes to design one in such a manner that oil workers in the field could easily take this vital measurement. We sold hundreds of thousands of these special tapes to an oil tool manufacturer imprinted with the company's logo.

Ordinary Force: tape measure
Extraordinary Result: tweaked it to special application for this unique industry.

15

Invest in haste
and lose your money in leisure.

We decided to manufacture pens in the European Common Market. Our Italian distributor was eager to partner with us using his facility in Turino, Italy urging us to move quickly to be ready for the trade shows in Europe.

Under pressure we made a hasty decision and equipped the factory. After a great deal of time and money was spent, we realized we were in the wrong place. Italian government attitude, labor unrest and escalating interest rates made it urgent for us to relocate. This time we did thorough research, found an ideal location in the south of France and, without setting an impossible deadline, were able to operate with much greater facility. Instead of throwing good money after bad trying to make the Italian operation work, we changed direction and were able to succeed.

16

The best products and services are designed by individuals.

One person with real talent will out perform almost any group. It has been said that a camel is a horse that was designed by a committee.

Just looking at a good product explains its function and utility. When explaining a service, the customer must understand the value within one minute.

Individuals designed some of our greatest leaps forward – telephones, airplanes, overnight delivery service and vanilla ice cream.

17

Product/service development can be a bottomless pit.

You have an idea for a product. You think it will be easy to make because you built the handmade sample in just a few days. Now you have to manufacture it economically and on a time schedule. When you are manufacturing a new product it always takes more time and money than you projected when you began. And sometimes it simply cannot be done. It also takes guts.

Your idea for a service business seems simple and needed. Set up your personal business where you are your only employee. You will know you are successful when you have developed a stream of income. At that point, if you want to grow the business, you will have the experience, ability and the funds.

18

Subcontracting is the cheapest form of manufacturing.

If you don't have a factory, now is not the time to build one. There is someone in the world with just the right plant and equipment to manufacture your product. He already has all the headaches of workers, unions, insurance, accidents, etc. You get a finished cost on which you know you can make a profit. This way you keep your fixed costs to an absolute minimum.

Necessary services such as invoicing, fulfilling, warehousing, secretarial can all be contracted.

We wanted to develop metal barrel ballpoint pens that looked like jewelry. We discovered that lipstick manufacturers could make this item for us with the equipment and personnel they already had. Today, it is even simpler...just use your search engine.

19

Keep it simple.

This oft-repeated truism must be applied to your product or service, its function and its design.

If you are making tape measures you don't need to provide a complete tool kit.

When providing caregivers for patients, it doesn't add to the earning power by the caregiver having an engineering degree.

One of my most productive sales executives sought my advice on a promotion for a major company. I was going through a long dissertation when he stopped me and said "Hey Boss, you are not going to pay me any more to get complicated, are you?"

20

Listen.
Think positive.
Project energy.

Immediately before an important meeting repeat this *basic* at least 3 times. This exercise prepares you mentally and emotionally to make the deal.

Early in my career I learned how to set myself up for important negotiations. Before going to the meeting, I would mentally rehearse the conversation that was about to take place. That preparation made me very effective at the actual meeting in responding to the other party. My rehearsal predicted the course of the conversation.

21

I gave it my best shot.
Now I must make it work.

Immediately after the meeting repeat this *basic* at least 3 times. With these words, give yourself a pat on the back with a reminder that there is still work to be done.

In 1976, I established a pen factory in the South of France. The French government promised us an incentive – for every job created they would pay us $150. They did not pay as promised and without that incentive, we were very short of cash. I went to Paris and confronted the head of the government agency. He told me the reason we did not get paid was the forms were filled out incorrectly. I said, "Show us the correct way to fill them out." They said it was too late for that. I gave them a friendly smile and said, "If we don't receive the promised funds, I will move the factory from France to Ireland." We received the funds.

22

If you can't explain your product or service in 30 seconds, you probably can't sell it.

You have 30 seconds to get your prospects' attention. If they don't understand you, you have lost the sale. Think of sending a text, not a letter. *Make every word count.*

We were very successful in selling custom jewelry – tie bars, money clips, and key chains – made in the shape of the customer's trademark. It took a lot of time to quote the cost of the stamping die, however they averaged $200. We vastly increased the sale by not making this an issue. We charged $200 for every die regardless of its complexity and could sell the idea without the complicated stamping die conversation.

23

If the premise is wrong, everything that follows is wrong.

If you think there is a big market for horse blankets (and this assumption is wrong), then you can manufacture the world's greatest horse blanket – and it will fail.

If you think there is a big market for blacksmiths (and this assumption is wrong), then you can shoe a horse but where is he going to go?

I was once asked to exhibit at a trade show on the premise that 75% of the ordering in that industry was done at that tradeshow. On checking it out, the 75% turned into 5%. The person that gave me the information had a vested interest in selling space at the show. It would have been a good buy at 75% of the market but at 5% it wasn't worth the time, the price or the effort.

24

Your business should be market driven – not product driven.

Product driven is trying to sell your product whether or not the public wants or needs it; *Market driven* means selling your product to the needs of the marketplace. *Product driven* almost killed the American automobile industry. *Market driven* made Apple dominant.

In providing a service, you *are* the product. Look to the marketplace to find what services are needed. Then, adapt your skills to fill that need.

25

Selling is one of the few professions with a built-in scorecard.

There is no place to hide. Either you made the sale or you didn't. When you work on commission, if you don't sell, you don't eat.

One of my salespeople had an extraordinary year and made more money on commission than I earned in salary as the president of the company. Fearing his commissions would be reduced, he was amazed when I congratulated him and paid him the full commission with the explanation, "the more he made the better off we all were." Beside that, one cannot argue with a deal that had previously been made just because it had been so profitable for the other party.

26

It's better to sell smart
than to sell hard.

The more you plan in advance, the more you learn of the prospect's needs – the more effective you are. There is nothing tougher than making cold calls without information about your potential client.

When banks were using premiums, our bank customers were amazed that we knew more about their regulations than they did. At that time banks offered a specific gift with the opening of an account of $1000 or more. But those gifts could only be within a certain value. Those gifts had to cost the bank less than $2.50 each. We sold them gifts that conformed to the banking regulations and opened the most accounts.

27

The best way to learn to sell is to go out and sell.

There is no substitute for actually doing it. The experience of being rejected may have more value than instant success. One must learn that rejection is not personal. Trial and Error are the two greatest sales instructors.

At a certain point in training our sales people, we had to say; "Now go out and do it". When asked how he became the first million-dollar salesman in our company, my brother explained, "I sell all the time." Even at the racetrack, he was selling and actually booked a great deal of his record sales while he was enjoying his favorite pastime, horseracing.

28

Features tell and benefits sell.

A customer wants to know what a product or service will do for him, not how it's made. Too much technical information can bury a sale. It's like asking what time it is and being told how a watch is made. A sale is closed only when the customer is convinced the product or service will do enough for him to justify the price he is paying.

A new supplier with a very large company addressed our sales force. He spent too much time telling us how big and strong his company was and how many people they employed. I stopped him in the middle of his pitch to say, "My sales force really wants to know how you can help them make more sales – not how big you are." He turned it around when he started again by pointing out the many ways that his products were superior and would sell easily.

29

It's easy to sell glamour, excitement, hope and feel good products. It's tough to sell insurance.

People are more likely to buy something that will make them feel good than to invest in protection against something that may or may not happen. If your product or service can offer instant gratification, you'll probably make an instant sale.

I once created a customer-copy-imprinted road flare to use in case of an accident on the highway. Theoretically it made sense, but in practice no one was ready to buy something that only came into play when their customer was in trouble. "Feel good" has more sales appeal than "feel safe."

30

Perceived value is what sells – real value is what repeats.

There is a real danger in convincing the customer that your product is better than it actually is. When it does not perform to expectations, you can forget about repeat business.

For years we manufactured ballpoint pens. The outside look is what caught the attention and made the sale. When we developed the best refill in the world with the greatest writing quality, the reorders came pouring in. Your product may look good, but it has to work great.

31

Sell the sizzle – but make sure there's a good steak underneath.

Good selling calls for presenting your product/service with excitement and glamour. You must create the impulse to buy *now*. But there is no way to have lasting success without constant quality.

When we produced trademark jewelry, a great deal of the real value was in the purity of the metal. Real sterling silver has the same look as silver plate. The genuine sterling silver will last a lifetime; the silver plate will tarnish and give away the fact that it was a cheap product. It is okay to sell silver plate, as long as you do not represent it as sterling silver.

32

The road to hell is paved with misrepresentation.

Abe Lincoln said, "You may fool all of the people some of the time, you can even fool some of the people all of the time but you cannot fool all of the people all the time." Business heaven is reached by telling it like it is.

I had a client that manufactured vitamins and food supplements. The sales force was trained to make all kinds of remarkable claims about the product being able to cure anything from insomnia to water on the knee. Their claims were subsequently proven to be false and they went out of business.

33

Honesty is not only the best policy; it's the most profitable.

There is no lie so ingenious that it will go undiscovered. After a thief is caught, he is never trusted. Every deal calls for a certain amount of trust. Being honest begets long-lasting relationships and creates better opportunities.

You can succeed in business without lying, cheating, or stealing.

We once had a competitor in the direct mail business that was continually undercutting our price. After we lost a lot of business, it was discovered that they had found a way to cheat the post office out of postage costs. Our competitor went bankrupt and we regained all the business that we lost, and more.

34

Build a better mousetrap and the world will beat a path to your door...as long as you have a good marketing plan.

Word of mouth is too slow a process in our instant communication world. As soon as you are ready, a strong advertising and marketing program must be launched before a competing product/service can get started.

We created a great employee-incentive program for a client. In order for it to be successful the client needed to continually publicize the program to their employees. The client said, "The program is so good it cannot fail." But the client failed to sell the program to their employees by not properly explaining its benefits. The program did not have a chance because nobody understood it.

35

Ask not how many people your advertising reaches, ask how many it sells.

Institutional advertising has fallen on lean times. What difference does it make how many people you reached? The important question is, "How many people were motivated to buy your product?"

When we founded our specialty advertising company in 1953, one of our major claims was that our client's entire advertising budget spent with us was on actual customers and prospects. There was no waste circulation. Today Google makes billions of dollars using the same principle.

36

The marketing program that worked in the past may not fly today.

There is no such thing as a formula that transcends time. Products and concepts become obsolete very quickly in today's fast changing market. If you are not current, you are extinct.

In 1953 the largest company in the sales promotion business featured exclusive calendars. Calendar advertising included everything from Norman Rockwell pictures to statistical information on specific dates.

Today there is no need to hang a calendar and, in most cases, no wall space on which to hang it. The computer obsoletes the old fashioned calendar. Jack Nadel International never depended on a particular item. Ideas that mean business never go out of style.

37

People talk thin and eat fat.

Finding the *real need* takes great skill. Everyone knows that carrots and broccoli are good for you, but they don't break sales records. Ice cream with high butterfat content sells like crazy.

The reason I love the pen business is that everybody needs them and does not have to be told how to use them. Throughout my career in the promotional advertising business I never got attached to one product or idea. Times change and market needs change with them. My thinking and merchandising constantly adapted to the present and the future.

38

A good deal is only good if it is good for everybody.

If it's good for one and bad for the other, it won't last. It is rare that anyone will come out of a negotiation with everything he wants, but the total deal must leave each participant in a better position.

In 1979 I made a licensing deal with Pierre Cardin. I needed a glamorous brand name for ballpoint pens we were manufacturing in France. We negotiated a license with Cardin. He designed the pens carrying his name and benefitted by gaining a completely new and reliable income stream receiving a royalty for every pen sold. We were able to manufacture and advertise a quality designer name product. Our distributors had an exciting new pen to sell that marked the first volume entry of a designer brand into the advertising pen business. The deal was good for everybody.

39

It's okay to lose a battle...
just make sure you win the war.

One of the biggest mistakes made by the amateur is not giving in on any issue. When the major points are finally discussed, he has already established a reputation for being unreasonable. Then the other side decides to get tough. Each side likes to think that it won. You must be more interested in getting what you want than being declared the "winner."

We were very successful with Pierre Cardin pens in Europe but did not have the license for the United States. We originally wanted the license for the entire world but backed off and settled for distribution in the European Common Market only. After two years of great success in Europe we were easily able to gain the license for the entire world. We lost the original battle for worldwide distribution but won the war when we finally got it.

40

Leave something on the table.

So many people think they must get the last drop of blood out of every deal. Victims have a way of coming back to haunt the victor. The more blood you took, the greater their determination to get even.

In 1957, when Japanese manufacturing had a reputation for poor quality, we made a deal with a Japanese manufacturer to produce a large quantity of high quality stainless steel flatware. After negotiating the best deal we could, I offered the Japanese manufacturer an additional 10% bonus to fulfill his promise of high quality. He was amazed, as no one before had ever offered to pay a premium for quality. I am convinced that by giving him something extra we were able to make this deal work.

41

Find ways to agree as early as you can in negotiations.

A negative start usually produces a negative result. A positive attitude at the outset indicates that you are reasonable and sympathetic to the needs of the other party. It sets the stage for getting over the thorny problems that are sure to come later.

Knowing we were facing stiff price competition in a negotiation for calendar cards for an insurance company, I decided to take a different tact from the start. I proposed a new idea to reduce the card's cost through cooperative advertising, where the insurance agent got his name imprinted on a quantity of cards and split the cost with the insurance company. By starting the negotiations showing the insurance company how much they could save by changing the distribution, we sold a larger quantity of cards.

42

Confront problems squarely.
They won't just go away.

Every deal has certain tough issues, and both sides are aware of these thorny problems. Pushing them to the side does not make the monster go away. Regardless of the topic being discussed, you still have to confront the 800-pound gorilla.

A major issue at a meeting of our board of directors was the salaries of company officers and how they related to each other. There were easier issues on the agenda, but I started the meeting with the statement that the salary problem had to be resolved before anything else was discussed. It wasn't easy, but it was finalized at the beginning of the meeting and we were able to proceed with other problems.

43

After you negotiate the best deal, give a little extra.

It is very important to end negotiations on a high note. The act of doing something nice that was not necessary creates enormous good will. It helps to ensure that the deal will be executed with the same spirit of cooperation that existed when the deal was made.

We leased a major piece of property after considerable negotiations. We had to make a number of alterations to suit the property to our needs. After the deal was made the real estate broker actually volunteered to provide an advisor to help, at no charge, to get the necessary construction permits. As an added good will gesture he gave us conversion tables and a construction kit as a move-in gift. This gesture opened the door to future business with this broker.

44

Always confirm your agreements in writing.

Most of what is said is forgotten soon after a conversation takes place. A written record dictated within minutes of the end of the meeting will preserve both the agreement and the spirit in which it was made. Years later, if there is any dispute, there will be no question as to what was said. It's a good idea to have the other parties sign a copy of the confirmation you send them, agreeing that this is also their understanding of the deal.

We made a deal to buy a large piece of property for our direct mail plant. Two weeks later we had a meeting to sign the papers. The owner's lawyer started to renegotiate. I was not interested in renegotiating but had nothing in writing. Because I had not immediately confirmed the agreement in writing and received a written confirmation, the deal fell apart.

45

An agreement is only as good as the people involved.

The most important element in any negotiation is the people with whom you're dealing. The character of an individual who has been in business for some time is easy to check. Any contract can be torn apart by a skilled lawyer – and there are lots of them out there waiting for the opportunity. Be on your guard.

I was introduced to a pen manufacturer who had a shady reputation but gave me a very low price on a large quantity of pens. The specification called for metal refills – plastic refills were available at a lower price. The pens were drop-shipped to our customers but one day someone gave one of those pens to me and, lo and behold, it had a plastic refill. That was their last order from us. When an individual has a shady reputation, he has usually earned it.

46

Never issue ultimatums.

The meekest and the weakest negotiators respond poorly when put in a corner. When you say, "this is my final offer," there is no room to back away. There are times when that is exactly the way you feel. But, before you utter these words, understand that you could be ending the negotiations.

In negotiating the merger of my company with a publicly traded company, the deal was made for an exchange of stock. There was also real estate involved for which they had agreed to pay cash.

As I was about to sign the contract they substituted their stock in exchange for the real estate saying, "Take it or leave it." Seeing me stand to leave they said, "You would blow this deal?" And I said, "Negotiations are over."

They backed off their position and we were able to make the deal where I kept the real estate and they paid rent.

47

No matter how tempted you are, do not bluff.

It's okay for poker. If you are called, you lose just the hand being played. In the real world of business, threats should never be issued lightly. Be prepared to execute any tough promises made... or don't issue the challenge in the first place.

At a very crucial time during our busiest season, my bookkeeper/office manager wanted to change all of our business procedures. After careful thought, I decided against her recommendation. She said, "If you don't do it, I will quit." While realizing it was a very bad time to be with out my office manager I said, "I accept your resignation and your last order is to write your final paycheck." She was astounded but it was the right thing to do for the company.

48

Try to end every break of a negotiating session on a high note.

It's not only okay, it is a good tactic to take a break when the situation gets tense and there seems to be no room for compromise. This gives both sides a chance to regroup and evaluate the situation. By ending a tough session with a humorous statement in good taste, or with some sincere compliment to the other side, you set the stage for a better attitude at the next meeting.

I was involved with a large printing plant losing money and could not find a way to stop the bleeding. The manager said, "If we put on a 3rd shift, we'll do better." I said, "If you do all the same things on the 3rd shift, we can manage to lose 33% more money. Take a break and we'll regroup in a half an hour." Everybody had a good laugh, the tension had broken, and the group came together again with constructive ideas that worked.

49

Keep the door,
and your options,
open.

No matter how strongly you feel that a failed deal is over forever, time has a habit of changing things. You always want to leave open the option of going back to the bargaining table at a future date.

I made an offer for a house in the Brentwood section of Los Angeles. The broker said the offer was too low. But when I remained firm the broker asked for a deposit. I immediately wrote a check, as this was a fantastic buy.

After hearing nothing for thirty days I contacted the broker. He said the offer was just too low and I requested he send back my check. However, I told him if at any time they wished to re-open negotiations, I would be available. Three months later the broker actually accepted my original offer.

50

Don't let your ego get in the way.

Examples of how inflated ego kill deals:

- You apply for a job and spend an excess amount of time telling your prospective employer how good you are. Instead, tell him how much good you could do for *him* and *his* company.
- You give yourself credit for more knowledge than you have and overstep your capability.
- A deal that you instigated is failing but you refuse to accept responsibility. Your ego does not allow you to admit your original mistake.

A successful executive retired but felt he could become even richer by online trading in the stock market. He lost his retirement fund and blamed the loss on the economy while never acknowledging his lack of trading skills.

51

All banks are not created equal.

Banks come in all sizes and descriptions. Never try to change them. It can't be done. Some are perfect for the small service companies. Others are slanted to big manufacturers. Still others build their services around the global market. Proper research will reveal the right bank for you. The choice is yours.

I wanted to buy back my company and several others. I knew I was out of my personal depth and needed help. My banker was just right. He planned with me the takeover strategy and then his bank financed it.

If I did not choose the right bank and the right banker at the right time, I could never have made the deal.

52

All interest rates are negotiable.

Not all customers of the bank get the same interest rate. Banks charge their most credit-worthy customers the prime rate. These are usually preferred accounts with excellent credit. It's up to you to negotiate the best rate they can offer.

This would also apply to terms. A bank's first proposal is not necessarily their best. It is perfectly okay to shop for a better deal. There are lots of banks out there, and one of them may just give you the deal you want or need.

Even more important – find the bank that has experience with similar business to yours.

We needed to increase our credit line. The bank decided to demand personal guarantees and raise the interest rate.

I invited another bank to give us a proposal. They gave us a lower interest rate and no personal guarantees.

53

A good banker does more than just lend money.

Making loans is the main business of most banks. Their traditional profit comes from borrowing money at one rate and lending it out at a higher interest. Banks can be a great source of information. They are in a unique position to check the personal reputation as well as credit of potential customers and suppliers. Whether your customer is local or global, your bank can supply information about their financial responsibility.

When we were exporting products to Europe and needed distributors, I used my international bank to recommend European prospects that were equipped physically and financially. As we were doing our due diligence (checking the facts), one of our most valuable sources of information was our bank. Many banks will not recommend but, when asked, will supply information on financial performance.

54

Volume is for ego.
Profit is what you take
to the bank.

When referring to a business, most people quote the gross revenues. There can be a wild variance in companies as to the net profit that's achieved. The question is not, how much can you *sell*, but how much can you *bank*.

A company decided to expand explosively. Through acquisitions and financial manipulation they went from revenues of $20 million to $600 million. Then they went bankrupt.

The important factor in their demise was a total attention to increasing the volume and insufficient planning to increase the profit margins in relationship to the increased overhead.

55

Bankers hate surprises.

Regardless of the problem, you must prepare your banker for any bad news so that they can be positioned to help as early as possible. The worst scenario is to run out of money and watch helplessly as your checks begin to bounce. At that point, it becomes almost impossible to do anything constructive. The last thing the bank wants to do is call in your loan.

When we upgraded our systems to computers to generate orders and statements, the new system broke down and threw everything behind including invoices and shipments. Realizing our problem, and knowing it would affect our cash flow, we informed the bank.

If we did not, we would be violating our loan agreements, and have enormous problems. By confiding, the bank cooperated and we got through a difficult financial crisis.

56

A good accountant is not just a scorekeeper.

A good accountant is your key to the whole bewildering world of finance. As a business grows, it gets more complicated. You are faced with the need to produce financial statements, projections, cash flow, and balance sheets. There is the constant demand from your bank, as well as your creditors, to convince them that you are solvent and a good risk. A good accountant will lead you through this jungle and keep you out of trouble.

While negotiating on a major piece of real estate needed to house one of our companies, I quickly realized that my regular accountant did not have enough real estate specific knowledge. So, we called in a real estate accountant. As he was well versed in this arena, he helped us solve the problems quickly and the deal was made.

57

Never talk to a tax examiner without your accountant present. Better still – Don't talk to him at all.

Tax people have a language all their own. Ordinary civilians can go bonkers trying to reason with them or even to understand why they are so intransigent. A good accountant understands the language and has the patience to deal with them. He may even get the tax guy to accept your position.

I made this mistake early in my career when a tax examiner decided we owed additional taxes. I found myself getting irritated and suddenly realized the reason. We were talking two different languages. I handled it badly and suffered the consequences. From that moment on I would only allow a professional tax accountant to present our case to any tax collecting agency.

58

You never know how good your accountant is until the IRS challenges your return.

There are few feelings that rival one's dismay when the notice arrives saying your tax return is being reviewed. Your accountant has to prove that all the deductions were correct. One never wins confronting the tax authorities. If damages are minimal, your accountant deserves a medal. If the results are a disaster, fire him.

When I interviewed my present accountant about income taxes, he said that overly aggressive accountants may save clients a lot of money in front but may cost them much more under examination. I told him that I was willing to pay whatever taxes were due and did not want to take questionable deductions.

The good news is that I have not had a tax conflict of any kind.

59

Lawyers and accountants, like taxi drivers, like to keep the meter running.

It is very much in order to check all the bills from your accountant and your lawyer. You are usually charged by the hour. It is up to you to decide whether all the time spent on your affairs was really necessary. Were you telling irrelevant stories and being charged $500 per hour for being sociable? It is almost impossible to get the details on all the time being charged. However, the mere act of questioning the charges keeps them down.

We were being sued. During a deposition the opposition attorney questioned me on some references I had made in a book that I wrote. It had no relationship to the case. The next month in my statement my attorney charged me an outrageous amount of money for having one of his assistants read my book. That was the beginning and the end of our relationship.

60

The chief function of your attorney is to protect and advise.

It's up to you to set policy and standards. Your lawyer's job is to tell you what you can and cannot do legally. Once you make a deal, he draws a contract that clearly states what you have agreed. You never really know how effective he is until the agreement is tested. Don't make your attorney responsible for your decisions. If you say, "My attorney won't let me do it," you are a wimp.

61

Tell your attorney everything before you get into trouble.

If you have even a remote feeling that something you did can have a negative legal consequence, discuss it with your lawyer. Even if that makes you look bad, tell everything without fear. It will be kept completely confidential. Basic law protects attorney/client confidentiality. He may come up with answers to your problems that may never have occurred to you.

62

An ounce of legal protection is worth a pound of lawsuits.

Almost always, the worst solution to a problem is a lawsuit. Schedule regular meetings with your attorney to discuss your activities. The complexity of your business and the amount of exposure should determine the frequency of these meetings. They can take place once a week, once a month, or once a year, whichever makes sense. If you can avoid just one lawsuit, it will have been time and money well spent.

When our business expanded internationally, I made sure that we had steady discussions with our attorney. Realizing that I was not knowledgeable in European law, on the recommendation of my bank, we retained an attorney who was an international specialist with a relationship in every other industrial country. In this manner we solved a lot of problems before they happened.

63

Try to settle all disputes out of court.

It takes great discipline to make unjustified concessions, but it is often the best course. Most juries in civil actions favor the little guy. If you are a wealthier/more powerful defendant than the plaintiff, you start with two strikes against you. The cost of litigation is usually far greater than the cost of an early settlement. Quite often, the only winners are the lawyers.

We caught a warehouse foreman stealing from the company. Confronted with the proof, he admitted his guilt. We fired him but did not bring any charges. Six months later he sued us for unlawful termination. We turned to our insurance company who promptly settled with him, paying him $10,000 to withdraw his lawsuit. When we questioned the insurance company payout they said, while he was guilty, it would have cost them $30,000 to defend the lawsuit.

64

Don't hire an elephant to kill a mouse... or a mouse to kill an elephant.

When you retain an accountant, lawyer, or outside consultant you need one just right for you. They come in all shapes and sizes. If starting a small business, select a small firm that can service your needs without excessive charges. As the business grows, the size of your problems grows, and the complexity increases. Then, get the best help you can. At that point, spending more can be cheaper in the long run. When starting, keep these expenses to a minimum.

We were faced with a lawsuit on an environmental issue involving asbestos. At first we made the mistake of using a large law firm. When I realized that we were losing we hired a small firm that specialized in this issue. We were able to resolve the case at a fraction of what the larger law firm was charging.

65

Think global – start local.

A good business may have worldwide potential, but you have to prove it first in your local area. If it doesn't work at home, it won't work on the other side of the world. Prove your deal first, then spread out.

I am often asked if I envisioned our international company when I started in 1953. The truth is, I put no limits on how big we would grow but never set a specific destination or timeline. In the back of my head was a global company, but on a practical basis I knew that it would only happen one step at a time as we acquired the knowledge and resources to expand successfully.

66

The right place to manufacture is where you get the best quality at the lowest price.

Consumers don't care where a product is made. While it may be politically correct to manufacture locally, consumers usually buy the best product at the best price. There are special cases where it is necessary to manufacture locally. This has more to do with the marketing than with the product.

At the beginning of my career I knew that we were part of a global market. When sourcing a product we had to compete with companies at the other end of the world. The real skill is manufacturing wherever they meet your price and quality standards. As a relatively small company we continue to survive by being competitive with factories around the world.

67

Seventy-five percent of the market for American merchandise is outside the United States.

After you have sold successfully in the local market, it is time to extend distribution across the country and then around the world. If you are competitive domestically, you will be competitive in the global market. It is not as complicated as you think to get international business.

We were manufacturing ballpoint pens in New York and were barely surviving due to intense competition. Through strong research we determined that our pens would find a big market in Europe. The right business plan was drawn up and within one year we were doing more business in Europe than in the United States. This moved us from survival to success.

68

A good idea has
no geographical boundaries.

There are very few businesses that cannot be expanded beyond the local market. A good concept or product can work anywhere in the industrial world. It may have to be adapted, but if it's successful around the corner, it will usually be successful around the world.

While working in Europe I discovered that a huge amount of expandable carry-on travel bags were being sold. The bag folded compactly and the traveler could open it up and use it at full size as he purchased more during his trip. Investigation told us that the bags were actually made in Hong Kong. We found the manufacturer and we became the first to import the expandable carry-on bag into the United States.

69

Adapt your products or services to the needs of each country.

It can be as simple as printing instructions in the language of each country in which you intend to sell, or as complex as changing the size or design to suit their standards. You cannot sell American cars in England unless you place the steering wheel on the right side.

I had the honor of serving on a Trade Mission to Japan at the request of President Ronald Reagan. The purpose of the mission was to increase the sale of American products in Japan. Among the other ten American businesspeople was the President of Winnebago. While traveling on a narrow Japanese road he asked why he Winnebago didn't sell in Japan. I suggested, "Either widen the Japanese roads or narrow the Winnebago." That was all it took for Winnebago to do business in Japan.

70

Never negotiate or sign a contract in a foreign language, no matter how well you think you understand it.

There are shadings to every language that are understood only by those who are born into it. Sometimes a certain inflection in the voice gives a word an entirely different meaning. Using an interpreter also gives you the advantage of a little extra thinking time before you have to respond.

I negotiated a licensing agreement with Pierre Cardin in Paris. When it came time to sign the contract, it was written in French. Instead of simply signing it, I insisted on an English translation, and then discovered a clause in it that was standard in Cardin's contracts but was incompatible to our deal. After discussion we came to an agreement on wording that worked for both of us. With a full understanding, we went on to a mutually satisfying relationship.

71

Taking a partner is like getting married.

The decision to acquire a partner has to be made with great care. It is a *business* marriage, and divorce can be just as costly and as painful as in real marriage. You may not love, honor, and cherish your partner, but you better make sure you respect them and that they are serving an irreplaceable function in the company.

When I created a new but very important company, I included the financial officer as a partner thinking at the time that it would be better for the company. I have since learned that professional people, accountants and lawyers, are very happy if you pay them a generous fee; you do not have to make them partners. As it turned out the inevitable separation was painful and, like most divorces, a good deal of money was spent on lawyers. In addition to the loss of money there was a great deal of aggravation.

72

All business is personal.

After all the facts are determined, the charts read, the computer printouts analyzed, a final decision is made. This is usually based not only on cold hard facts but also on the decision maker's personal feelings. No one will buy a bad deal from a good guy, but people always try to do business with those whom they like and trust. This particularly applies to service businesses where personal contact is constant.

When I engineered a leveraged buyout (buying a company with its own assets) from a failing conglomerate, a great deal of the bank's financing for the deal depended on my personal relationship with the president of the bank. And when he asked me why the bank should make the loan to me personally rather than the conglomerate I answered, "Who do you think will most likely fulfill the commitment?" He looked me right in the eye and said, "You got the deal. Your personal guarantee is enough."

73

Trust your gut.

Sometimes instinct is referred to as a mystical element through which many decisions are made. Your gut instinct is really the sum of all your experiences. When you have a feeling that a deal is either right or wrong, trust it. It will usually be the right decision.

Very early in my career I was offered a participation in a deal based on the Mexican government subsidizing the use of silver in Mexican products. In 1950 the silver content in a Mexican silver tray was worth more than the cost of the tray. I was told that by simply melting down the tray and extracting the silver, the silver could be sold on the commodities market for a handsome profit. My gut told me this was a bad deal because melting the tray served no purpose other than to take advantage of a misuse of the subsidy. The Mexican government withdrew the subsidy when they realized their mistake. Those that invested in the deal suffered a great loss.

74

There is no such thing as a stupid question or a stupid idea.

When people are afraid to ask a question or suggest a new idea, progress is inhibited. An inquiring mind, properly encouraged, is a tremendous asset. One never knows from which direction the next great idea will come.

For three years we had built a big market for a low priced Schaffer pen in Europe. Due to it's outstanding success, Schaffer decided to distribute it themselves leaving us needing a name brand writing instrument. Suddenly my wife said, "You're wearing Pierre Cardin Jeans. Let's make a deal with Pierre Cardin to design a new pen and license the name." I said, "His reputation comes from clothing not from stationery. However, let's think... Can we make it work?" It turned out the name was strong enough to sell and we made a very good deal with Cardin that opened up new business in licensing.

75

Money attracts good people, but pride makes them great.

Everyone needs to be motivated to produce over and above what is expected. A feeling of pride creates an invigorating climate in which to work.

Forty years ago we created a sales incentive program for our account executives where those that achieved certain goals came to be called Golden Tigers. Earning the status of a Golden Tiger became very desirable because it included extra bonuses and a special trip where all the Golden Tigers enjoyed being together over a long weekend. Winners were not only proud of themselves but took enormous pride in the accomplishment of their peers.

76

Competition breeds innovation and is usually good for everyone.

A free market is the healthiest arena for business. Your competitors make you rise to the need. New products and lower prices for the consumer are the natural results. Without free competition, the economy is doomed to fail and governments can fall. Remember the Soviet Union.

For years IBM towered above all competition in the computer business. When Apple, Dell, and Hewlett Packard challenged the giant with new and innovative products and services, it expanded the market for everybody. When the consumer has many choices the whole world benefits. Open competition forces all companies to do better.

77

Careful planning is more important than hard work.

It is in the nature of most hard-driving businesspeople to work hard. However, strategy will ultimately dictate success or failure. It's very difficult to retrieve a mistake once it's committed to action. Review the details over and over again. Then go for it.

A simple process, like planning in person sales calls, can save a great deal of time and increase efficiency. A salesman once complained to me that he was working too hard, so I reviewed the calls that he was making and found that he was driving great distances between sales calls. By better planning and simple geographics he increased his sales by over 100%. Time is your most productive asset and it cannot be recovered.

78

Someone who knows more than you do is not necessarily an expert.

Many people confuse intellectual knowledge with practical expertise. An expert is someone who has been successful *and* has real experience. All consultants are not experts.

We decided to target the savings and loan industry where a great deal of advertising money was being spent particularly on premiums. We made tremendous progress when we hired a salesman who had been an executive at a savings and loan association. He knew their regulations and understood their specific problems from practical experience. Using his expertise he was able to create premium campaigns that bought in new savings accounts.

79

You don't have to be an S.O.B. to be a success in business.

It was the legendary baseball coach Leo Durocher who said, *nice guys finish last*. But if you examine the records, he didn't finish first too often himself. Respecting the dignity of others has never been a deterrent to success.

When I hired my brother Marty as a salesman I was aware of the fact that he was the nicest guy I knew. He was totally honest and had many friends. This "nice guy" broke all sales records and replaced me as President of the company. Despite the belief that nice guys finish last, this one finished first. Being honest, open and trustworthy is a very big asset in even the toughest of businesses.

80

Your decision will not change the course of history. Lighten up.

There is a tendency to place too much importance on every move that is made. By agonizing over each decision, you give the impression of being insecure. Then, when you have a major decision to make, it is difficult to establish that this one really *is* important.

In the early days of Jack Nadel International our biggest producer of business agonized over every decision. His intense detail work sometimes clouded his real accomplishments. He worried endlessly about making the right move. Everybody involved in processing his orders dreaded the time they would spend on them. I would often say, "Lighten up. This will not solve the world's problems."

We could not change him. He was affected physically and passed away at an early age.

81

Truly understanding the problem is halfway to the solution.

Problems do not get solved when the central issue is avoided. Continuing difficulty almost always points to people rather than things. When you recognize the cause, the solution may not be pleasant, but it is obvious. Understanding the problem can be very complicated, take your time.

We acquired an advertising agency that headquartered in New York. One of the reasons it was losing money was their executive expense accounts. Their lunch meetings started with three martinis. I spent several hours with the company president explaining how essential it was to reduce the expense accounts. Then my chief financial officer created a plan of checks and balances. Nothing worked and it finally dawned on us that the culture and character was almost impossible to change. Reluctantly, we had to close down the operation.

82

Do not resist change.

Over the years, repetition produces a comfort level. Time and changing business conditions have a tendency to make old methods obsolete. Despite the discomfort, procedures have to be altered to meet new circumstances.

Our bookkeeper could never get her work done within the eight-hour day. So I asked her, "What is your most time consuming operation." She answered, "Checking credit. For every new order, I check their bank and two trade references by phone." I asked how many accounts did she reject for bad credit over this past year. She answered none. "OK," I said, "From now on do not check any credit for orders under $500. Just automatically approve them without explanation." The result: we suffered no credit loss and she was able to all her work without overtime.

83

Without hard work,
talent is wasted.

If you are not prepared to make the effort, you negate your prospects for success. Thomas Edison once described *genius* as being 90% perspiration and 10% inspiration.

We purchased at a very low price an established brand pen company and discovered why they were losing money – their refills were inferior. We patiently checked every refill on the market and found that we could buy the best refill made for much less money than it cost to manufacture our own. So, we closed the refill department and, with a lower cost, produced a quality pen. Then we made it very profitable by adding global distribution.

84

Work with people who know more than you.

Insecure employers hire people who will not challenge them. The more real talent that surrounds you, the greater the chance they will help expand your business.

When we decided to go into the export market I hired a brilliant veteran who was totally familiar with export trade. He spoke eight languages and had grown up in different parts of Europe. The fact that he knew more than I did about the European Common Market opened the door to areas previously unknown. I was able to operate very profitably using his knowledge.

85

Confidence breeds success and success breeds confidence.

The more you do, the more you know you can do. You attempt to reach greater heights each time you reach your goal. With each victory you are more sure of the next one. It is a wonderful and rewarding circle.

The first steps in business are scary. It gets easier as you grow. My method of growing the company was to proceed from one arena to another. Each time it's like advancing the pieces on a chess set, the more you move the better you are equipped for the next move. Expanding my business from Los Angeles to San Francisco was a major move that taught me a great deal. With that success it was much easier to go across the country and then global. Being successful in the first stages of business equips you mentally and financially to make the next leap.

86

A business either goes forward or it goes backwards.

There is no such thing as a nice, comfortable place. Time and competition do not allow it. When a company does not grow, it begins to atrophy, and failure is inevitable.

Brown and Bigelow was the biggest company in the advertising specialty business in 1950. When there was very little competition, they dominated the market but only with exclusive products — calendars, playing cards and selected desk items — that they themselves manufactured. The arrival of many competitors with multiple product lines left them unable to compete until they modified their business plan. In 1953 I founded my company selling the best products available that carried our client's message and were able to win a good part of the market.

87

The inability to make decisions can destroy a company.

Business becomes paralyzed when decisions are not made in a timely fashion. The window of opportunity does not remain open indefinitely. If you don't act, your competition will.

We discovered a unique expandable travel bag. Before anybody had seen it in the United States we seized the opportunity by importing a large quantity from the Orient and were the first to introduce it and got the lion's share of that business. The timing was perfect as the following year it dropped in price. As more importers entered into the market we quietly moved out.

88

A meeting that is not planned is usually wasted.

Take the time to create an agenda that systematically attacks problems and explores opportunities. Set them in a logical sequence as stepping-stones to a final resolution. There is no such thing as an orderly meeting put together in a disorderly fashion.

In 1968 a large publicly traded company acquired Jack Nadel International. I took a post as a group vice president and had to attend a number of unplanned, frustrating meetings. At one point I had to ask, "Exactly what are we trying to accomplish with this meeting?" I felt as though I was in a ship going around in circles. Every meeting must have a reason and a goal.

89

A mistake made once is human. The same mistake made twice is stupid.

Most companies can survive almost any mistake. But a company has to fail when the same mistake is made over and over again. We should learn more from what we do wrong than from what we do right.

We caught a warehouse manager stealing merchandise and selling it on his own. When we confronted him he confessed and we agreed to not prosecute but terminated his employment. A year later he sued us for unlawful termination. The mistake I made was not prosecuting thereby leaving the company vulnerable to a lawsuit.

90

A reputation
is usually well earned.

Con men are charming and convincing. The deals they offer are both logical and sensational. Take the time to check out their reputation. Try to find third parties with whom they have done business. If the trail is strewn with disaster, pay attention and pass.

The interesting part of a relationship with a con man is that he becomes totally likeable if not loveable. I met this brilliant individual at a trade show in Milan, Italy. He spoke ten languages fluently and part of the problem was that he sincerely believed he was right and just. It was certainly a mixed experience but I got burned when he sued me for what he felt I should have paid him and had no problem leveling false charges. He was really like the cow that gave Grade A Milk and then kicked over the bucket. I was lucky he didn't destroy the entire barn.

91

The trip to success is as much fun as arriving at the destination.

The joy of life should never be postponed for the chance of eventual success. Each step along the way must bring some form of gratification. No one has a passport that states how long he or she is going to live. Every step in the pursuit of success should be as much fun as achieving it.

I can honestly say that I have never spent a boring day in pursuing my career. More importantly, I even enjoyed those hours of uncertainty between creating and executing a deal. One of the secrets is to recognize the humor in every situation. The true enrichment comes from the friendships that are formed.

I once had a problem in Europe and when I mentioned it to a client from Belgium he told me he would fly to meet me the next day to help in any way he could. When he couldn't get a flight, he drove from Antwerp, Belgium to Cannes, France just to help me. This reinforces my basic idea that all business is personal.

92

Deals are like buses.
There is always another one
behind the one you just missed.

Don't despair when you lose a deal that you really thought you wanted. Most often, it is followed by another proposition that is even better than the one you thought you could not do without.

I was negotiating the purchase of a building to house our direct mail company. When we were in the process of closing the deal, there was a series of misunderstandings. At the last minute I decided that there were too many obstacles for it to work. I felt sad that the other side was inflexible and the deal fell through. The very next day I received an offer from another broker for a property that was actually superior and that we bought. Everything about the deal that we consummated was better than the deal that we lost.

93

Pass on your secrets
to the next generation.

Over the years you created your own methodology for success. Your approach may not be the traditional methods taught in business schools, but it worked for you. If you are proud of what you accomplished, then teach it to others. You can be responsible for improving the quality of someone else's life while you give yours more meaning.

This is my motive in writing this book. My great desire is to pass on what I have learned to as many people as possible that can benefit from my experience. They say, "You can't take it with you." This applies even more to ideas than to money. One of my greatest joys is when I witness the success of people that I have mentored.

94

Age and senility do not
go hand in hand.

Staying involved is the key to a full life. As long as you are current, you are young. Many octogenarians have something important to say. Listen.

Throughout my long career I have witnessed the effects of aging and changing conditions. In our modern society we don't give enough credibility to experience. Sometimes this situation is precipitated when an older person does not accept new ideas and technology. And conversely, powerful professional advice is in danger of being ignored when a younger executive does not take advantage of counsel by an experienced old pro.

I seek to encourage older people to embrace new methods. The principles of good business are constant; the tools that are used are constantly changing. Regardless of age, we must always reinvent ourselves to meet changing conditions. I can no longer travel around the world for personal meetings but the Internet has made it possible and practical to conduct business with anybody from the comfort of my own home.

95

The harder I work,
The luckier I get.

We all get equal doses of good luck and bad luck. The truth is nothing good happens or is appreciated if you do not work hard to achieve the goal.

Earlier I told the story of how we thought of licensing the Pierre Cardin name to design and brand a special pen for us in Europe – a deal that proved to be very successful and exceeded all expectations. Years later I heard the story about how lucky Jack Nadel was because he and Pierre Cardin happened to be in the same place at the same time. To set the record straight – luck had nothing to do with it. We targeted Cardin choosing from a field of prominent designers. The only reason we came together at this particular time was because the concept, the business and the location all came together through diligent research and planning.

96

The world judges me on results and not on how hard I work.

Great results take intense effort. The marketplace doesn't care how much time you spent creating the product or service. Talking about working hard makes you weak.

I previously told the story of how we discovered the wristband calendar — one of the most profitable items we ever made. But a great deal of hard work went into making it the product it eventually became.

When we decided to manufacture the wristband calendar we spent hundreds of hours designing presentation packages. The original product came to us with the 12 calendars packaged in a clear plastic case. We designed packages either by the month, by the quarter, or by the year tailored to different industries. We had a package for pharmaceutical manufacturers, automobile dealers, insurance companies and banks, and subscription services. Nobody cares how hard you worked; they are only interested in success or failure.

97

Stress to success.

Making money can be very stressful. Don't fight it. Accept it and embrace it. There is a price for everything we get, particularly financial rewards. Enjoy the process and you will enjoy the end results even more.

At the age of 35 I was experiencing great gastric discomfort and was diagnosed with a peptic ulcer. A specialist prescribed a diet of creamy soft food. When the ulcer got worse, I consulted with my family doctor. After asking several questions he said, "The cause of your illness is one word — stress. If you are aggravated by every decision, it doesn't matter what you eat. It will all turn to acid. You must understand that you make each decision with the best information you have, then, just let it go."

I took his advice and the peptic ulcer completely disappeared within six months. You cannot change the stress in business; you can change your attitude.

98

Silence is golden.
Listen, learn, and prosper.

When making a deal, first listen and learn what the other side _really_ wants. Now it is up to you to give it to them. You only know what your prospect wants when _they_ state it clearly. You have two ears, two eyes, and one mouth. Use them in that order.

One of my good customers was a good-sized manufacturer. As part of my sales presentation, on the first call I asked him what was his biggest problem. Usually the answer to that question from this kind of company was sales or I need to develop new products. He looked me in the eye and said, "My biggest problem is safety. We have too many accidents, our insurance costs have gone through the roof, and I personally agonize when one of our workers is severely injured."

I presented this customer with a complete safety program with incentives and special awards for injury free performance. I was able to help solve his problem but I would never have been successful with this account had I not asked for and **listened** to his real problem.

99

Fear strikes out.
When you negotiate in fear,
you lose.

All deals must be made when you are completely confident in your position. You have a much better chance of getting what you want when you are willing to walk away if it doesn't happen. Don't even start to try to make a new deal if the counter-offer will be a disaster for you and you have no place to go. It is better to make no deal than a bad deal.

We were negotiating a new credit agreement with our bank. In preliminary conversations I stipulated that I was no longer willing to put up my personal guarantee and said definitively that if the agreement called for my personal guarantee, I would not sign it. After a discussion they agreed to my condition. Two weeks later they came to my office with the newly drawn agreement that called for my personal guarantee insisting that they decided not to give us a new credit line without it. I stood up and said, "Gentlemen this meeting is over. You are no longer our bank." A month later I signed an agreement with another bank, without any personal guarantees.

100

**If I give you a dollar,
and you give me a dollar,
we each have a dollar.**

**If I give you an idea,
and you give me an idea,
we each have two ideas.**

By sharing with others we increase our own capacity. By giving to others we do not take something away from ourselves. The only competition that exists is our desire for excellence.

If you have an *idea* that has worked for you,
let us share it on our website:
www.ideasthatmeanbusiness.com.

Glossary of Business Terms

Balance Sheet – A financial statement that summarizes a company's assets, liabilities and shareholders' equity at a specific point in time.

Cash Flow – A measure of a company's financial health. Equals cash receipts minus cash payments over a given period of time.

Conglomerate – A corporation that is made up of a number of different, seemingly unrelated businesses.

Credit line – An arrangement in which a bank or vendor extends a specified amount of unsecured credit to a specified borrower for a specified time period.

Due Diligence – The process of investigation, performed by investors, into the details of a potential investment, such as an examination of operations and management and the verification of material facts.

Financial Statement – Records that outline the financial activities of a business, an individual or any other entity. Financial statements are meant to present the financial information of the entity in question as clearly and concisely as possible for both the entity and for readers. Financial statements for businesses usually include: income statements, balance sheet, statements of retained earnings and cash flows, as well as other possible statements.

Gross Revenues – The total amount of money received by the company for goods sold or services provided during a certain time period.

Incentive Program – A formal plan used to promote or encourage specific actions or behavior by a specific group of people during a defined period of time. Incentive programs are particularly used in business management to motivate employees, and in sales in order to attract and retain customers.

Licensing – The granting of permission to use intellectual property rights, such as trademarks, patents, or technology, under defined conditions.

Net Profit – Often referred to as the bottom line, net profit is calculated by subtracting a company's total expenses from total revenue, thus showing what the company has earned (or lost) in a given period of time (usually one year).

Personal Guarantee – Promise made by an entrepreneur which obligates him/her to personally repay debts his/her corporation defaults on.

Prime Rate – Interest rate charged by banks to their largest, most secure, and credit worthy customers on short-term loans. This rate is used as a guide for computing interest rates for other borrowers.

Projections – A quantitative estimate of future economic or financial performance.

Jack Nadel is an international entrepreneur, founder of Jack Nadel International, a worldwide leader in the specialty advertising and marketing industry. He has written books, lectured on business at colleges and universities, and had his own television show (*Out of the Box with Jack Nadel*) in Santa Barbara. Jack flew 27 missions as an Air Force B29 navigator and was decorated with the Distinguished Flying Cross and the Air Medal with 3 Oak Leaf Clusters. Since retiring he continues to mentor future business leaders. Jack authored three business books – *Cracking the Global Market, There's No Business Like Your Business* and *How To Succeed In Business Without Lying Cheating or Stealing* – as well as a novel – *My Enemy, My Friend*. At age 87, Jack leads a robust, full life writing, mentoring and savoring every moment.

Index of 100 Basic Ideas

Confidence breeds success and success breeds confidence. 85

Confront problems squarely. They won't just go away. 42

Deals are like buses. There is always another one behind the one you just missed. 92

Do not resist change. 82

Do your own research. 9

Does it work? Will it last? Who wants it? 13

Don't fall in love with your idea. 7

Don't hire an elephant to kill a mouse… or a mouse to kill an elephant. 64

Don't let your ego get in the way. 50

Fear strikes out. When you negotiate in fear, you lose. 99

Features Tell and Benefits Sell. 28

Find a need and fill it. 1

Find ways to agree as early as you can in negotiations. 41

Great design is when ordinary force produces extraordinary results. 14

Honesty is not only the best policy… it's the most profitable. 33

I gave it my best shot. Now I must make it work. 21

If I give you a dollar, and you give me a dollar, we each have a dollar. If I give you an idea, and you give me an idea, we each have two ideas. 100

If the premise is wrong – everything that follows is wrong. 23

If you can't explain it in 30 seconds, you probably can't sell it. 22

Invest in haste and lose your money in leisure. 15

It's better to sell smart than to sell hard. 26

It's easy to sell glamour, excitement, hope and feel good products. It's tough to sell insurance. 29

It's okay to lose a battle, just make sure you win the war. 39

Keep it simple. 19

Keep the door, and your options, open. 49

Lawyers and accountants, like taxi drivers, like to keep the meter running. 59

Leave something on the table. 40

Listen. Think positive. Project energy. 20

Money attracts good people, but pride makes them great. 75

More deals die from sloppy execution than from bad concepts. 5

Never issue ultimatums. 46

Never negotiate or sign a contract in a foreign language, no matter how well you think you understand it. 70

Never talk to a tax examiner without your accountant present. Better still; don't talk to him at all. 57

No matter how tempted you are, do not bluff. 47

Pass on your secrets to the next generation. 93

People talk thin and eat fat. 37

Perceived value is what sells – real value is what repeats. 30

Product/service development can be a bottomless pit. 17

Scale your business plan to fit your ability to finance it. If funds are limited, take it in stages. 10

Self-motivation is the key to success 2

Sell it before you commit to making it or doing it. 12

Sell the sizzle – but make sure there's a good steak underneath. 31

Selling is one of the few professions with a built-in scorecard. 25

Seventy-five percent of the market for American merchandise is outside the United States. 67

Silence is golden. Listen, learn, and prosper. 98

Someone who knows more than you do is not necessarily an expert. 78

Stress to success. 97

Subcontracting is the cheapest form of manufacturing. 18

Take calculated risks. 3

Taking a partner is like getting married. 71

Tell your attorney everything before you get into trouble. 61

The best products and services are designed by individuals. 16

The best way to learn to sell is to go out and sell. 27

The chief function of your attorney is to protect and advise. 60

The harder I work, the luckier I get. 95

The inability to make decisions can destroy a company. 87

The marketing program that worked in the past may not fly today. 36

The right place to manufacture is where you get the best quality at the lowest price. 66

The road to hell is paved with misrepresentation. 32

The three R's for successful business 4

The trip to success is as much fun as arriving at the destination. 91

The world judges me on results and not on how hard I work. 96

There is no such thing as a stupid question or a stupid idea. 74

Think global – start local. 65

Truly understanding the problem is halfway to the solution. 81

Trust your gut. 73

Try to end every break of a negotiating session on a high note. 48

Try to settle all disputes out of court. 63

Understand your strengths and weaknesses. 6

Volume is for ego. Profit is what you take to the bank. 54

When looking for advice, talk to someone who's done it successfully. 8

Without hard work, talent is wasted. 83

Work with people who know more than you. 84

You don't have to be an S.O.B. to be a success in business. 79

You never know how good your accountant is until the IRS challenges your return. 58

Your business should be market driven – not product driven. 24

Your decision will not change the course of history. Lighten up. 80

My Ideas